YOU
HAVE
WHAT IT
TAKES

How to Finally Start Making
Your Dreams a Reality

DR. JEVONNAH ELLISON

WESTBOW®
PRESS
A DIVISION OF THOMAS NELSON
& ZONDERVAN

WestBow Press books may be ordered through booksellers or by contacting:

WestBow Press
A Division of Thomas Nelson & Zondervan
1663 Liberty Drive
Bloomington, IN 47403
www.westbowpress.com
1 (866) 928-1240

ISBN: 978-1-4908-5934-7 (sc)
ISBN: 978-1-4908-5933-0 (hc)
ISBN: 978-1-4908-5935-4 (e)

Library of Congress Control Number: 2014919957

Printed in the United States of America.

WestBow Press rev. date: 01/06/2014

The information contained in this guide is for informational purposes only.

I am not a lawyer or an accountant. Any legal or financial advice that I give is my opinion based on my own experience.

The material in this guide may include information, products, or services by third parties. Third-party materials are comprised of the products and opinions expressed by their owners. As such, I do not assume responsibility or liability for any third-party material or opinions.

The publication of such third-party materials does not constitute my guarantee of any information, instruction, opinion, products, or services contained within the third-party material. The use of recommended third-party material does not guarantee any success and/or earnings related to you or your business. Publication of such third-party material is simply a recommendation and an expression of my own opinion of that material.

No part of this publication shall be reproduced, transmitted, or sold in whole or in part in any form without the prior written consent of the author. All trademarks and registered trademarks appearing in this guide are the property of their respective owners.

Users of this guide are advised to do their own due diligence when it comes to making business decisions, and all information, products, and services that have been provided should be independently verified by your own qualified professionals.

This book is dedicated to my incredible
Mom, my angel on earth
Dr. Rezine Keng

You taught me the meaning of love and gratitude. You never gave up on me, and you always told me that I had what it took to reach the top. This one's for you. I love you with all my heart.

Being confi dent of this very thing, that He who has begun a good work in you will complete it until the day of Jesus Christ.

—Philippians 1:6 (NKJV)

Hear, my son, and receive my sayings,
And the years of your life will be many.
I have taught you in the way of wisdom;
I have led you in right paths.
When you walk, your steps will not be hindered,
And when you run, you will not stumble.
Take firm hold of instruction, do not let go;
Keep her, for she is your life.
Do not enter the path of the wicked,
And do not walk in the way of evil.
Avoid it, do not travel on it;
Turn away from it and pass on.

—Proverbs 4:10–15 (NKJV)

Jesus answered and said to him, "Because I said to you, 'I saw you under the fig tree,' do you believe? You will see greater things than these."

—John 1:50 (NKJV)

Praise for *You Have What It Takes*

"This is not just another feel-good book. *You Have What it Takes* asks the hard questions to help us find our best purpose AND take action to make that a reality. Lady J reminds us, Yes we are all called – but we still have to decide to take action to fulfill that calling. This book will move you from "I can" to "I will.""

Dan Miller, Author New York Times bestselling 48 Days to the Work You Love

www.48days.com

"This book is a blueprint that will guide you into reaching life's accomplishments. It will help you understand how complete you are and how to use your God-given gifts to be successful without giving up. Lady J shares the hard work, pain, and sacrifice that made her complete, and she will give you confidence in knowing that success can happen for you."

—Presiding Bishop Charles E. Blake Sr.

www.westa.org

"This book will accelerate your efforts to push towards your destiny! *You Have What It Takes* by Dr. Jevonnah Ellison is a scholarly endeavor that will create an enthusiastic surge of possibility for your future. She outlines an achievable blueprint for your goals as each chapter accelerates your efforts to push toward your destiny!"

—**Dr. Barbara McCoo Lewis,** Assistant General Supervisor, Church of God in Christ Worldwide
www.socalcogicwomen1.org

"Your book just glows with personal enthusiasm and advice that can light a fire under readers who want to step out and live a life of purpose and success!"

Christine Moore
The Editor

"Jevonnah ("Lady J", as you will soon know her) implores us that "You are needed. You are the answer to someone's question and the solution to someone's problem. Your value is of immense worth." *"You Have What It Takes"* is simply a powerful read, one that will most assuredly become one of your life's "hinge moments".

~ **Chuck Bowen**
Business Coach | Entrepreneur Strategist
www.ChuckBowen.net

"If you have big dreams and you keep finding yourself stuck and unsure about how to move forward; this is the book for you. Dr. Ellison guides you through the process of creating the life you were made for. Her inspiring and practical approach will give you the courage and resources to keep charging ahead when you're tempted to give up. A must read for aspiring entrepreneurs."

Michael McGreevy
The Pursuit of Authentic Manhood
www.berealmen.com

"If you are stuck and lack the confidence to do great things, read Lady J's book! She lays out an inspiring framework to take the next step."
—Darryl W Lyons, Author Small Business Big Pressure.

Darryl W Lyons, ChFC, CFP(R), AIF(R)
Chief Executive Officer
PAX Financial Group, LLC
www.PAXFinancialGroup.com

"I think you have done a fabulous job with your book. It's inspiring, motivational, and honest. Even as a Successful business man, Lady J reminded me about some of the most important keys to Success and how to stay there. Thanks Jevonnah!"

Dr. Rafael A. Perez
"The UberGooder"
http://ubergoodexperience.com

"Jevonnah does a masterful job at inspiring the reader as well as asking them to look inside themselves to find the motivation to become their best self. She asks the tough questions, but those questions always help lead to massive success. If you are looking at getting unstuck, then I highly recommend this book for its practical advice and helping you with introspection so you will say "why not me?" as you move towards the next level of success.

Jeff Long
www.TrueFocusMedia.com
Podcast: OnlineCourseCoach.com - Helping you master online courses and creating a community of raving fans.

"Lady J shows us how we are all Divinely built to serve with passion and carves out a path to becoming authentically you— if you dare to take action!"

Jeff Beaudin
LaunchPOINT - Career Coaching and Development
Certified 48Days Coach
Certified Teamability® Consultant
www.frompassiontopaycheck.com

"In *You Have What it Takes*, Jevonnah masterfully guides you through discovering your true passion and positions you to turn that passion into your reality. If you've been looking for a book that will not only inspire you, but also provide practical strategies for achieving your dreams, look no more."

Nick Pavlidis
www.FiveMinutesWithDad.com
www.ATerribleHusband.com

"Embrace your purpose, dream big, and live a life that matters. In *You Have What It Takes*, Lady J shows you how."

Greg "GD" Lengacher -
Author, Surviving Divorce: Your Guide To Finding Hope And Healing After An Unwanted Divorce
www.survivingdivorcepodcast.com

"Jevonnah is a master encourager and that encouragement runs through every page of her new book. If you have a goal, even one that you don't dare whisper in an empty room, this book will help you give it wings. Jevonnah reminds us that we are needed. We are the answer to someone's question and the solution to someone's problem. And once we get unstuck, we are unstoppable. Step into your place of greatness with *You Have What it Takes*."

Emily Chase Smith, Esq.
Author, Speaker and Business Financial Coach
www.EmilyChaseSmith.com

"One phrase kept resonating with me as I read through *You Have What it Takes*, "The unstuck are unstoppable." That is powerful. Those aren't just words to Lady J, it is what she believes and how she lives, but most of all it is what she really wants for you. Get unstuck and be unstoppable - *You Have What It Takes*."

Diana Bader
Owner, Youth Coach, Fresh Canvas, LLC

CONTENTS

FOREWORD

For several years, Jevonnah served as my administrative assistant. I observed her many wonderful qualities and the character that caused her to become the wonderful woman of God and Bible teacher that she is now. Even then, her potential for what she would become was manifested.

Her book is a blueprint that will guide you into reaching life's accomplishments. It will help you understand how complete you are and how to use your God-given gifts to be successful without ever giving up.

In this book, she shares the hard work, pain, and sacrifice that made her complete, and she will give you confidence in knowing that success can happen for you. A dream is not complete without a vision, and a vision is not complete without becoming a reality.

One of the most difficult tasks in life is to value your worth. At the end of this reading, your self-image will improve, your decisive measures will increase, and your boundaries will decrease. This will lead you to believe positively in yourself, to believe that no challenge is too hard for you and God.

Bishop Charles E. Blake, Sr.
Senior Pastor, West Angeles Church
Presiding Bishop, COGIC, Inc.

PREFACE

I'm so glad and honored that you chose to read this book. I am confident that if you are inspired by the principles within these pages and will put them into action, you will begin to experience the massive success that I know God has destined for your life. This book was birthed out of a desire to see people experience success in every area of their lives and reach the top. It is my goal that you, after reading this guide, will begin to see just how capable of extraordinary accomplishments you really are.

Recently, I began to see and talk to many people who had great dreams and ideas but just didn't know how to put those ideas into action. They needed a plan, a blueprint, and a proven way of creating something unique and original. The problem was this: although they had great dreams and visions, many wouldn't do anything about them. Maybe the reason for their inaction was fear, indecision, or doubt. Maybe it was even a lack of confidence in their own God-given gifts, talents, and abilities. No matter what your reason is, I'm here to remind you that you do in fact have what it takes to accomplish your biggest goals. *You just have to start.* You see, being stuck is no longer an option. The unstuck are unstoppable. Let me explain.

I'll never forget running my very first marathon. As I ran the long journey of 26.2 miles, I learned from my experience. I learned not to sprint the first mile, which was what it felt like I was doing. I was just excited and happy to finally be doing something that I'd always said I'd do. It was a beautiful California day, the sun was shining, and twenty-five thousand happy runners were everywhere. (Well, maybe not all of them were happy, as most of us were in pain!) The energy of the marathon was electric.

I learned a valuable lesson that day: to never compare my beginning with someone else's finish. What does that mean? It means that you have to run your own race of life. If you run a twelve-minute mile and someone else runs a six-minute mile, don't beat yourself up or compare yourself. Each of you will reach the finish line at your appointed time. We go wrong when we try to run someone else's race. There is nothing more beautiful than your being *authentically you.* Having the courage to be yourself and to really be okay with it starts with confidence.

Now, thirteen marathons later, I get joy and excitement out of running my own race and helping so many others along the way to run theirs.

Let's make one thing clear. You are different, extraordinarily different. Whether or not you know it or feel like it, you have what it takes to succeed when others give up and quit. You were born with a set of unique talents, skills, abilities, and gifts. There is no one like you. Sure, there are times when you may want to give up too, but you don't. Rest, yes. But quit? Never. Amateurs give up when they don't hit a home run. Pros keep swinging until they do.

A word of caution: this book is not about a quick, surefire way to have an easy, hassle-free life. Rather, it's about hard work. It's about *diligence*. It's about *commitment*. It's all about the pain, sacrifice, and pure determination it takes to get to a place of greatness in your life. You have a message to share. Your voice matters. The world is waiting. It's your time.

So sit back, relax, grab a cup of warm goodness, and enjoy this book. It's a quick and powerful read that you can probably get through in one sitting. If at any point while reading this guide you have any questions, please don't hesitate to contact me. You can best reach me by accessing my website (www.

jevonnah.com) or my Facebook page (www.facebook.com/
jevonnahellison). Even if you don't have any questions, I'd
love for you to come by and say hello! Enjoy! I am praying
for your incredible success.

Jevonnah "Lady J" Ellison
Dr. Jevonnah Ellison
Your Leading Purpose Strategist & Leadership Coach
www.jevonnah.com

1

Why Not You?

You have big dreams. People need the message and special gifts that only you have. The world is waiting for *your* voice. Why can't you be the one to start a business, write a book, or even be the first in your family to achieve a major accomplishment? Too often we doubt ourselves and wait for the validation of others before we decide to do anything significant. If you decide to wait on the approval and acceptance of other people before you start building your dream, you'll be waiting a long time. The time for you to start is *now*. You can't afford to waste any more time. Build, lead, and achieve. Decide now to do something great with your life.

I'll never forget a message I heard by my spiritual father, Presiding Bishop Charles E. Blake several years ago entitled, "Why Not You?" He encouraged believers to remember and to hold fast to Philippians 1:6: "Being confident of this very thing, that He who has begun a good work in you shall perform it until the day of Jesus Christ." And that is the foundation Scripture for everything you will read in this book. Never forget that you are capable of amazing victories and that through Christ you really can do all things. "I can do all things through Christ who strengthens me" (Philippians 4:13).

2

The Confidence Factor

Confidence is freedom from doubt, a belief in yourself and your abilities. Confidence drives business. To be in the driver's seat, you must believe in your ability to make things happen. Otherwise, you are just along for the ride.

—Marshawn Evans, *Skirts in the Boardroom*

Know that you have the ability to shape your confidence. As you launch your business, step into your purpose, and find your voice, realize that another person's opinion about you is never as important as *your* opinion about you. You can rise to *any* challenge if you have the right frame of mind. It's amazing what you can see when you choose what not to look at. People often say what they're going to *start* doing in a new season, but what are you going to *stop* doing? How about putting off fear and replacing it with faith? What about rejecting doubt and starting anyway? If you try to start when you're "ready," you may never be ready. You have to start now. It's your season.

Protect your confidence. What you rehearse is what you perform. Rehearse the outcome in your mind. Confidence creates transference of belief. You are capable!

Another person's opinion of you cannot define you without your permission. Too many times we allow other people's opinions to stunt our growth and success. My business (Jevonnah Ellison Leadership Coaching LLC, www. jevonnah.com) was born out of a desire to help high-potential people break out of the mundane and ordinary and leap into the extraordinary, to help them become unstuck—because the unstuck are unstoppable. I have seen many leaders with great potential, but they just kept getting stuck. Perhaps they were battling loneliness, were tired of being misunderstood and cast aside, or were fearful of stepping out into their true life's purposes. Some were lawyers, but they really wanted to be consultants. Some were ministers, but they really wanted to open their own businesses. Some had no clue about what they were supposed to be doing, but they were miserable in their current nine-to-five jobs. Yes, it's time for you to step up to the plate.

But do you have the skills, knowledge, and systems to even hit the ball? You've got to equip yourself with the right tools, systems, and strategies to excel and reach the top. Take inventory of the people you're hanging around. Jim Rohn— the great philosopher, American entrepreneur, author, and motivational speaker—once said, "You are the average of the five people you spend the most time with." Make sure that the company you keep pours life into you, not drain it.

You are needed. You are the answer to someone's question and the solution to someone's problem. Your value is of immense worth.

3

Courage to Conquer

A main function of purpose is courage. A strong sense of purpose motivates you to step outside the box. You will never win the games that you don't play. You will never make the shots that you refuse to take. Success is a product of the decisions you make, the risks you take, the networks you generate, and the opportunities you create.

In his timeless classic, *The Strangest Secret,* Earl Nightingale reminds us that we become what we think about. Our thoughts influence our self-image—how we see ourselves. Do you see yourself as a risk-taker? As a believer? Your self-image influences your courage. Your courage influences the actions you take. The risks you take reflect the rewards you reap. Courage is simply the alignment of your self-image with your purpose.

At the end of the day, excellence requires constant, consistent, and confident steps of faith. Many are called, but few are chosen. The chosen ones are those who choose to answer the call.

Purpose is your *compass*. It gives you guidance and direction.

Purpose is your *conviction*. Through establishing your values and standards, it protects you from crossing boundaries. "You teach people how to treat you by what you tolerate."

Purpose is your *courage*. It drives you to strive for excellence, motivates you to dream, and enables you to take risks.

Finding your purpose is not as hard as most people think. Purpose is what drives you. It's what makes you passionate. It's not some elusive phenomenon that you can never grasp. Because you were created on purpose to live with extraordinary purpose, you are supposed to know what your purpose involves. The sooner you realize that, the sooner you walk with direction. You need to acknowledge the purpose you possess. And only you hold the key. Here are some questions to help you align your purpose:

- What do you like to do?
- What do you *not* like to do?
- What are you good at?

- What do others say you're good at?
- What motivates you?

One of the questions I get asked the most is: "How do I know my purpose?"

Have you ever asked that question, too?

Do you ever wonder what you're really supposed to be doing with your life? Perhaps you feel like you've been living without a sense of purpose for sometime or perhaps even a few years now.

Many times, it's easy to get caught up living someone else's purpose for your life that you neglect to live your own.

I want to give you 3 of the easiest ways to get clear on your purpose. These ideas will help you punch fear in the face and finally start living the abundant life you were meant to have.

#1 Start asking yourself better questions

To get clarity on your purpose, ask yourself these 3 questions:

What are my unique skills and abilities?
What are my personality traits?

What are those dreams and passions I have that keep showing up over and over again?

By asking yourself better questions, you'll get better answers and be on the road to clarity of your purpose. What do you really want out of life? How can you help others in a way that no one else can? Once you can answer these questions, you'll be well on your way and ahead of most everyone else.

#2 Craft a personal mission statement

In the book, Wisdom Meets Passion, by New York Times Bestselling Author, Dan Miller, and his son, Jared Angaza, a resource for crafting a personal mission statement is provided. (Order the book at www.48days.com) Spend at least 2 hours working through the steps to have clarity of your purpose and a plan of action.

In Dan's words: "You cannot expect success to show up or to have any sustained passion without knowing your purpose."

#3 Get better company and take action

If you want to be successful, you need to spend time with people who are already successful. Invest your time reading quality books, strengthen your prayer life, and listen to educational podcasts that will elevate your thinking. Learn something new everyday. And then – don't just learn it, but take action on what you learn. You can take action now by getting and listening to The Millionaire Clarity Pack (available at www.jevonnah.com) – an inside look into the purpose of 4 successful entrepreneurs who will help you get the crystal clear clarity you need to get started. And if you've already started walking in the direction of your purpose, the Clarity Pack will help you maintain and accelerate your momentum.

In the November 2014 Issue of Success Magazine, Tom Corley, author of Rich Habits: The Daily Success Habits of Wealthy Individuals, describes a 5-step process for knowing your main purpose.

He wisely says, "Odds are, if you are not making sufficient income at your job, it is because you are doing something you do not particularly like. When you can earn a sufficient income doing something you enjoy, you have found your main purpose."

Here's the 5-step process:

1) Make a list of everything you can remember that made you happy.
2) Highlight those items on your list that involve a skill, and identify that skill.

3) Rank the top 10 highlighted items in the order of joy they bring to you. Whatever makes you happiest of all gets 10 big points.

4) Now rank the top 10 highlighted items in terms of their income potential. The most lucrative skill of all is worth 10 points.

5) Total the two ranked columns. The highest score represents a potential main purpose in your life. Presto!

Remember Psalm 37:5: "Commit thy way unto the LORD; trust also in him; and he shall bring it to pass."

4

The Resistance

In his bestselling books, *Do the Work* and *Turning Pro*, Steven Pressfield talks about something called "the Resistance." Resistance is that enemy we all face when we get ready to do something great. Doubt, fear, apprehension, or your inner critic—or just the sheer difficulty of a project—can make resistance raise its ugly head. The key is to start anyway. Start before you're ready, and realize that you can outsmart the resistance if you just keep working and refuse to give up.

Rule of thumb: "The more important a call or action is to our soul's evolution, the more resistance we will feel in pursuing it" (Steven Pressfield, *Do the Work*, 2011).

5

What on Earth Are You Here For, Anyway?

So, let's get right to it.

Do you know what you're really supposed to be doing with your life? Are you doing that thing right now? Do you know your life's purpose?

I know, I know. These are boring and tough questions, right?

Well, if the honest truth be told, some people don't have a clue what they're really supposed to be doing. Instead, they let other people and circumstances dictate how their lives should be. Many float aimlessly through life without any real goals, direction, or vision. Too many people work jobs they hate with people they don't like, only to get up the next morning and do it all over again.

I don't want that to be you. Instead, I want you to live. I want you to reach the top. I want you to live a life of brilliance, productivity, and passion. My goal is for you to live a life that truly honors and exemplifies your love for God.

Do you still not know exactly what you're here for? Well, keep reading, and let me ask you a few questions:

Question 1: What comes easy to you? In other words, what do people compliment you about that you just shrug off as nothing? (If you actually take time to answer these questions, you'll get so much more out of this book.)

_____

_____

_____

Question 2: What would you do for free if you never got paid?

_____

_____

_____

Question 3: What good thing(s) can you *not* stop doing?

_____

_____

_____

Grab a blank sheet of paper. If you haven't done so already, write down your answers to the questions above. (You may also use the space for notes provided at the back of this book.)

Now, some people will follow through on this, and some people won't. We read about what we need to do. We hear about what we need to do. But when the time comes to actually do it, most of us hesitate. Or we get busy and are distracted. Perhaps we are just too comfortable where we are. There's a story about an old dog who was sitting on a front porch moaning and whining. One day, a friend of the owner of the dog came by and said, "Why is that dog whining so much?" The owner of the dog said, "Oh, he's lying on a nail". The other man said, "Well why doesn't he just get up and move?" The owner said, "Well I guess it just doesn't hurt bad enough."

Don't let that be you. Take action and do something to activate your dreams today.

You might not have answers to all of these questions, but hopefully you've got at least one or two. If you've managed to answer all three, bravo!

Next, turn the paper over. Write down five ways you want to serve other people. Why are we doing this? *Because your life's purpose is rarely just about you. It's about helping, serving, and giving to other people in some way.*

To help you get started, I'll share my own list of "Ways to Serve Other People":

1) Offer weekly encouragement through Bible study lessons
2) Write a book
3) Produce quality content from my business, Jevonnah Ellison Leadership Coaching, LLC, complete with coaching programs, workshops, masterminds, products, and services
4) Empower professional women to live a life of integrity through my virtual network, *Professional Women of Integrity*
5) Prayer line conference calls
6) Daily encouragement via social media, podcasting, and webinars

After this simple but thought-provoking exercise, I came to learn that I was in the business of transformation. I was put on earth to transform lives through the power of Christian coaching/mentorship and the gospel message of Jesus Christ. Allow me to introduce myself:

"Hello, my name is Dr. Jevonnah Ellison, better known as 'Lady J' to many, and I am in the business of transformation. As a Leading Purpose Strategist and Leadership Coach, I equip high potential women and visionary men with confidence and clarity so that they can live out their God-given purpose. I help women create lives of authentic purpose, happiness, and integrity through the power of entrepreneurship and personal development.

Philippians 1:6 is the foundation for all I do: 'Being confident of this one thing, that He who has begun a good work in you, shall perform it until the day of Jesus Christ.'"

Now it's your turn. This time, you fill in the blanks.

"Hello, my name is _____ _____, and I am in the business of _____. I help X (people) do Y (action) so that Z (outcome)." This is what is otherwise known as your value proposition. Your value proposition is unique to you and should be a reflection of your most authentic self.

Your life matters, my friend. Go and do something *big*. As Steve Jobs would say, put a dent in the universe. Leave a legacy. Start today. You can do this. Let's go!

6

Where to Begin

So, you've made up your mind that you want to live a life of excellence. You've decided to actually do something about it.

Congratulations! You're ahead of the majority. Only a small percentage of people who say they're going to do something actually follows through. You have a mentality of excellence, and with that "rich" mind-set, you can do so much. I thought it'd be interesting to share these facts with you.

On his website, RichHabitsInstitute.com, Tom Corley, best-selling author of *Rich Habits*, outlines a few of the differences between the habits of the rich and the poor.

1) 70% of wealthy people eat less than 300 junk food calories per day. 97% of poor people eat more than

300 junk food calories per day. 23% of wealthy people gamble. 52% of poor people gamble.

2) 80% of wealthy people are focused on accomplishing some single goal. Only 12% of the poor do this.

3) 76% of wealthy people exercise aerobically four days a week. 23% of the poor do this.

4) 63% of wealthy people listen to audio books during their commute to work versus 5% of poor people.

5) 81% of wealthy people maintain a to-do list versus 19% of the poor.

6) 63% of wealthy parents make their children read two or more nonfiction books a month versus 3% of the poor.

7) 70% of wealthy parents make their children volunteer ten hours or more a month versus 3% of the poor.

8) 80% of wealthy people make "happy birthday" calls versus 11% of the poor.

9) 67% of wealthy people write down their goals versus 17% of the poor.

10) 88% of wealthy people read thirty minutes or more each day for education or career reasons versus 2% of the poor.

11) 6% of wealthy people say what's on their mind versus 69% of the poor.

12) 79% of wealthy people network five hours or more each month versus 16% of the poor.

13) 67% of wealthy people watch one hour or less of TV every day versus 23% of the poor.

14) 16% of wealthy people watch reality TV versus 78% of the poor.

15) 44% of wealthy people wake up three hours before work starts versus 3% of the poor.

16) 74% of wealthy people teach good daily success habits to their children versus 1% of the poor.

17) 84% of wealthy people believe that good habits create opportunity and good luck versus 4% of the poor.

18) 76% of wealthy people believe that bad habits create detrimental luck versus 9% of the poor.

19) 86% of wealthy people believe in lifelong educational self-improvement versus 5% of the poor.

20) 86% of wealthy people love to read versus 26% of the poor.

So you see, you're not ordinary. You're not average. Being wealthy is so much more than just money. It's about your attitude and disposition towards life. Your life matters more than you think.

Toxic Charity by Robert Lupton talks about the way people in third-world countries view poverty. Here is a list of his top ten items (with number 1 being the most frequent) that make people poor:

10. Lack of good thoughts
9. Not sharing
8. Not having money to buy food
7. Not knowing God
6. Broken relationships
5. No hope or belief in self
4. Isolation
3. Not being able to make progress
2. Not knowing your strengths and abilities
1. An empty heart

So, now the question is, where do we begin? How do we live this life of excellence?

Reading great books is an excellent place to start. Three great ones to start off with are *No More Dreaded Monday*s by Dan Miller, *Platform* by Michael Hyatt, and *Start* by Jon Acuff. A complete list of reference books is available on my website at www.jevonnah.com.

Check out these quotes about reading great books:

"When you sell a man a book, you don't sell him twelve ounces of paper and ink and glue—you sell him a whole new life."

—Christopher Morley

"Books are the main source of our knowledge, our reservoir of first faith, memory, wisdom, morality, poetry, philosophy, history and science."

—Daniel J. Boorstin, Librarian of Congress Emeritus

"The books you read today will fuel your earning power tomorrow."

—Tim Sanders

"When I want to read a good book, I write one."

—Benjamin Disraeli

"When you write from the heart, you not only light the dark path of your readers, you light your own way as well."

—Marjorie Holmes

"A book should serve as the axe for the frozen sea within us."

—Franz Kafka

Many people work jobs they hate with people they don't like only to get a paycheck that barely helps them survive. Now, not everyone is in this boat, but if *you* are, keep reading. Even if you aren't in that group, keep reading. There's something for you here too.

Many of us don't pursue what we love doing because of two main things: *fear* and *ignorance*.

Fear

Fear doesn't get loud until you start doing work that matters. It doesn't get loud until you actually start putting a dent in the universe. The higher you go, the more visible you become, and the more opportunity there is for critics to judge and nitpick. You have to punch fear in the face.

However, remember the wisdom of the Word when dealing with criticism. All criticism isn't bad. Sometimes we need to hear it, and it can help us grow in understanding.

"Whoever disregards discipline comes to poverty and shame, but whoever heeds correction is honored" (Proverbs 13:18 NIV).

"Whoever heeds life-giving correction will be at home among the wise. Those who disregard discipline despise themselves, but the one who heeds correction gains understanding" (Proverbs 15:31–32 NIV).

"Whoever remains stiff-necked after many rebukes will suddenly be destroyed without remedy" (Proverbs 29:1 NIV).

The first step is to identify what you're actually afraid of. Write it down. Share it with your close friends and those you trust. You'll probably be surprised to learn that others face the exact same fears. In 2 Timothy 1:7, the apostle Paul said, "God has not given us a spirit of fear, but of love, power, and a sound mind."

Ignorance

What do you want to do? Have you written it down? Do you want to write a book? Start a business? Lose weight? Land a new job? Then you have to do some work.

Educate yourself. Read books. Talk to experts in your chosen field. Volunteer. *Leaders are perpetual learners.* You never stop learning. When you stop learning, you stop growing. Don't be afraid to ask questions and admit, "I don't know" if you don't have the answer. But then be fully committed and determined to find out the answer. Refuse to allow ignorance to stop you from reaching your goals. Hosea 4:6 says, "My people perish from a lack of knowledge."

Identify what you want to do.

Write it down. If you don't already have a journal, get one. Use it frequently. Write down your goals and dreams and how you plan to accomplish them. Marshawn Evans, a life catalyst and marketplace mentor, often says, "Where there is no action, there is no traction." Review your journal weekly to make sure your mind stays fresh with the new thoughts and ideas you've come up with.

Call out your fears.

Then refute your fears with truth. For example, you may be saying, "It's too late for me. My time has passed. I'm not smart enough, and I don't have enough money."

Here's the true statement you ought to say: "It's too late for fear to stop me now. Success comes to me easily. I never give up. God has given me a creative mind to think of ideas and ways to generate income. I will walk in the truth of Philippians 4:13: 'I can do all things through Christ who strengthens me.'"

Identify the tools you need to make your dream a reality.

Try getting up an hour earlier tomorrow morning. Work on your dream. Read. Research. Invest in yourself. Hire a coach. Ask questions. Educate yourself. Make progress every day, and before you know it, you will have come further than you thought was possible in just one or two months.

What are you going to do right now to get started?

_____

_____

_____

_____

_____

_____

_____

_____

_____

7

Your Defining Moment

So, I'm sitting down today to write for thirty minutes straight. I'm actually looking forward to it. As a "Leading Purpose Strategist and Leadership Coach," I love writing, reading, and learning. I recently read a book by Jon Acuff called *Quitter*. In it he talks about "hinge moments." A hinge moment is when something significant, big or small, happens in your life. It's a hint, an open door to your true purpose and destiny. It's a clue to what you're supposed to be doing for the rest of your life. Let me explain and give you a real-world example.

One of my hinge moments happened for me at nine years of age. I have an amazing mom who has always believed in me. She constantly supports, encourages, and prays for me. Having her support and love has made all the difference in my level of success and love of wisdom.

While growing up, my sister (age 14) and I (age 9) didn't watch much television. My mom, a retired college instructor, had a different beat for us to march to. This was our after-school routine:

- have a snack
- read at least one chapter of the Bible (I was 9, so of course I looked for the shortest chapters!)
- write a one-page "Bible Report" on the main points and do homework
- do light chores
- help prepare dinner and eat
- read or watch at least thirty minutes of current events, and write a summary of what we learned (This was for extra credit.)
- enjoy family time
- clean up and get ready for tomorrow
- pray and enjoy more family time
- go to bed

Did every day go smoothly and right on schedule? Of course not. But here's the deal: Mom instilled in us the amazing gift of learning, writing, and growing every day. We weren't sitting in front of the television all afternoon watching mindless nonsense. Instead, Mom was all about developing our minds and making us into women of character. Of course, she let us have our fun too. We went to the movies, played sports, and did fun stuff like any other family. But when it was time to be about business, Mom was serious, and we knew it too.

I have her to thank today for so many things. Even though I didn't appreciate it at the time, and I tried to find the widest-ruled paper I could to avoid writing so much, I knew Mom was setting us up for something big. And today that something big has turned into an incredible love for leadership, writing, personal growth, and sustainable success.

It's like Earl Nightingale once said years ago: "We become what we think about." Because our minds had wholesome material going in, positive results came out. My sister went on to get full scholarships, travel to the White House, and even cheer for the Lakers with the Laker Girls. And this was all before she even graduated from high school. It was amazing!

Here are three strategies you can use, starting now, to get smarter in just thirty minutes a day:

Strategy 1: Turn off the television. Look, you'll never develop your mind if you're constantly feeding it trivialized drama. There is a time and place for appropriate entertainment, but when you're trying to get smarter, turn off the television and read a book for thirty minutes instead.

Strategy 2: Listen to podcasts. One of the fastest paths to personal growth and development is in listening to people who are doing what you want to be doing and learning from them. I have found podcasts to be an amazing resource of tools, tips, and strategies in my business as a leading purpose strategist and leadership coach. Turn your car into a rolling university, and listen for at least thirty minutes, depending on your drive. Here are some of the podcasts I listen to on a regular basis:

- *This Is Your Life* by Michael Hyatt
- *48 Days to the Work You Love by Dan Miller*
- *The Charged Life by Brendon Burchard*
- *Internet Business Mastery by Jeremy Frandsen and Jason Van Orden*
- *Ask Pat by Pat Flynn*
- *Smart Passive Income by Pat Flynn*
- *The Ray Edwards Show by Ray Edwards*
- *EntreLeadership by Dave Ramsey*
- *Online Marketing Made Easy by Amy Porterfield*
- *The Portfolio Life by Jeff Goins*
- *The Dave Ramsey Show*

Strategy 3: Get a coach. In his book, *The Compound Effect*, Darren Hardy says, "I have always found it interesting that the most successful people, the truly top performers, are the ones willing to hire and pay for the best coaches and trainers there are. It pays to invest in your improved performance." It pays to invest in your improved performance. Even the former CEO of Google, Eric Schmidt says, "one thing people are never good at, is seeing themselves as others see them. Having a coach really, really helps." A coach will help you go further, faster. To learn more about my one-on-one coaching in less than ten minutes, go to www.jevonnah.com

A hinge moment for me was the realization that I could actually become a successful author, and today I love to write. Time stands still for me when I read, teach, write, learn, and grow. I could do it all day, within reason, and not get overly tired. That's how much I love it. That's how I know my passion and purpose. Writing those childhood reports taught me three quality principles that have helped shape my character and life today: discipline, character, and determination.

Another significant hinge moment happened for me when one of my best friends, Collette Johnson, died on Christmas Eve of 2013. We were friends and worked together for nearly 13 years. She was beautiful, smart and full of God's love. The cancer took over so fast. She got sick in September and at the young age of 42, died on Christmas Eve just 3 months later. I promised her family that I would run the 26.2 mile LA Marathon in her honor. I did, and crossed the finish line with tears thinking of her. I realized upon crossing that finish line that I had to do everything God was calling me to do. Even if I didn't have all the answers or resources, I couldn't put it off any longer. Tomorrow isn't promised. Plus I knew that I had to be about God's business for my life if I wanted to see her again. Collette did so much good with her life. She had many dreams and hopes that were fulfilled. But they never would have happened if she didn't decide to "start".

So, what's your hinge moment?

Right now you may be doing work that you're not really into—or perhaps even hate. But what is the one thing that you would do for free if you never got paid? What do people say you're good at that you brush off and dismiss when they compliment you?

You have a voice. You have a story. The world needs to hear it. Will you have the courage to step through the door of your opportunities? It all starts with a small, simple "hinge."

Take action: what two things are you going to do in the next thirty days to progress in the direction of your goals? Write them down.

8

How to Live a Life That Matters

Everyone wants to live a life that means and stands for something. Everyone should want to impact the lives of others in a great and lasting way.

What will people say at your funeral (or your "homegoing," as we say in the church about one who has accepted salvation)? What regrets will you have when you come to the end of your journey? How can you start living a better life now?

These are heavy questions. If we don't take the time now to answer them and live a life of purpose and intentionality, we could wind up just drifting through life like so many others who are content to live a life of mediocrity.

This book is not for small-minded people. It's not for the mediocre. It's not for bystanders. Rather, it's for world changers—dreamers, risk takers, leaders, and key players.

Living a life that matters is important to people like you. You understand that life is not all about you. You've somehow tapped into that secret reservoir called servanthood, which ultimately leads to leadership. You understand that to lead is to serve.

I challenge you today with three principles, which you may, in fact, already know. But even if you do know them, let them serve as a gentle reminder to tell you this: "Be not weary in well doing, for in due season, you shall reap if you faint not" (Galatians 6:9).

Principle #1: Dedicate Your Work to God

Let's face it: every day won't be perfect. There will be people who make life difficult for you, intentionally or not. If you own a business, you might have to fire employees from time to time. (That's why it's wise to be slow to hire in order to get the *right* people on the *right* bus in the *right* seat the first time around. Thanks, Jim Collins! bestselling author of *From Good to Great*)

Every day won't be a bowl of cherries. But if you do your work as if you're doing it for God, you can never go wrong. God knows your heart and understands the real reasons, intentions, and motivations for everything you do. Give your business, your work, and your life back to God. You'll never regret it. "Whatsoever ye do, work heartily, as unto the Lord, and not unto men" (Colossians 3:23).

Principle #2: Dare to Work Your Passion

This is a big one. So many people are working at a job they tolerate, but they're desperate to break free and pursue their dream job. To that I say, "Blossom where you're planted— until the door opens for you to pursue your dream job." You'll have to take the consistent, disciplined action needed to walk through that open door.

No job is perfect. Every single one will present its own share of problems. Yes, work your passion. But first, identify it and find connections between where you are now and where you eventually want to go.

Principle #3: Forgive One Another

If you're going to live a life that matters, you've got to start forgiving people. Life is too short to hold on to grudges and carry bitterness in your heart. Be the bigger person and forgive. When you hold unforgiveness in your heart, it's like you're drinking poison while waiting for the other person to die. Don't do it. Learn to let stuff go. We all get hurt, but you do not have to let unforgiveness define your life.

A true leader understands the power of forgiveness and practices it. A great resource to help you with this is a book called *Let it Go* by Bishop T. D. Jakes.

Action Steps

Write down two steps you are taking—or are going to take—right now to help you live a life that matters. The more practical and specific you can be, the better. For example, you can say things like: "I am going to start praying in the morning at 5:30 for fifteen minutes" or "I am going to start eating whole foods and go to the grocery store this weekend to stock up on more fruits and vegetables."

_____

_____

_____

_____

_____

_____

_____

_____

9

Don't Miss This Important Secret to Achieving Your Goals

So, how do you actually set a goal and keep it? Michael Hyatt, *New York Times* best-selling author of *Platform* and former president of Thomas Nelson Publishing, introduced me to SMART goals. A smart goal is:

1) Specific: Your goals must identify exactly what you want to accomplish with as much detail as possible. For example, instead of saying, "I want to write my first book," say, "I will write the table of contents for eight chapters of my first book by the end of the week."

2) Measurable: You can't manage what you can't measure. Try to quantify the result. You want to know for sure if you hit your goal or not. For example, instead of saying, "I want to earn more money this

year," say, "I will earn $25,000 more this year by taking on a part-time job."

3) Actionable: Every goal should start with an action verb—like *run, finish, stop*, and so on—rather than a to-be verb like *am, be,* or *have*. For example, instead of saying, "I am going to work out," say, "I will run a mile per day."

4) Realistic: A good goal should stretch you, but you have to use common sense. If your goal is within your comfort zone, perhaps it's not big enough. For example, instead of saying, "I want to qualify for the Boston Marathon," say, "I will train five days a week to increase my running speed by one minute per mile."

5) Time-Bound: Every goal needs a date associated with it. When do you plan to deliver on that goal? It could be midyear or the beginning of the year. A goal without a date is just a dream. Make sure that every goal ends with a "by when" date. For example, instead of saying, "I need to lose thirteen pounds," say, "I will lose thirteen pounds by December 25 by eating less and exercising more."

And remember to write things down. Maybe you can tell by now that I'm a huge fan of journaling. This is critical. There is power in writing your goals down. When you write something down, you are stating your intention and setting things in motion. Turn your goals into tasks by taking bite-size pieces of your goal and then doing meaningful work daily in the direction of your goal. Three great applications to help you with this are www.todoist.com, www.wunderlist.com and www.habitlist.com.

Review your Goals

Review your goals frequently. Changes happen when you review your goals on a consistent basis. At the beginning of each day or sometimes the night before, I go through my journal of goals and notes to remind myself of what I set out to do. Then I ask myself, "What's the next step I need to take to move toward this goal?" *The key here is to let your goals inspire your to-do list.* And if you've completed a goal, celebrate! Take time to reflect on all the hard work it took to achieve your goal. Give God all the glory.

Be careful who you share your goals with. Try not to share them with people who are not committed to helping you achieve them. Instead, share them with people who will support you and sincerely pray for you. P.S. And make sure they can genuinely celebrate with you without reservation when you actually achieve those goals!

10

Do It Scared

I told myself that I was going to start writing. Every day. For at least thirty minutes. I was going to write and share what was on my heart, and then, when the thirty minutes was up, I was going to stop. It's amazing to me how taking this small step has impacted my writing journey.

I'll be honest with you. Writing your first book is challenging to say the least. It's one thing to write a manuscript when you're the only one who sees it. It's a completely different thing to launch your manuscript for the whole world to see. (I'm glad you're here!)

I'll never forget an article I read by best-selling author Seth Godin in which he talked about writer's block. I paraphrase, "There is no such thing as writer's block. Just write poorly every day until you get better. In other words, do it scared."

That struck a chord with me. There I was thinking that my writing had to be perfect before I published it on my blog or in a book. Nothing could be further from the truth. *People want real, authentic, raw truth.*

There is nothing quite as liberating as just being yourself. It comes with being comfortable enough in your own skin to break out of the box, shake off the familiar, and dare to do something great.

Talk and write about the bumps and bruises you've gotten along the way. Tell how you wanted to quit but didn't. Show that you can encourage others to reach their destinies, even when all manner of drama is going on in your own life.

Do it scared. You don't have to be great to get started, but you do have to start to be great.

Start the business scared. Start the idea scared. Chances are, if you're waiting for the moment when you're not scared or don't have any level of hesitation, you'll never do it.

The fact is that you, my friend, have to *start*. Go and do something great with your life. You have what it takes. Do work that matters. Put a dent in the universe. Leave a legacy. *You can do this.* If no one else tells you, let me tell you: I believe in you.

11

There's Something Greater for You

I teach a ladies Bible study at my church called *Wise Women Build*. The women who attend are an amazing group from all walks of life, who know what it means to push, persevere, and make it through the hardest times of life. I admire and thank God for them often.

We all go through rough spots in life. We all have setbacks. Some of us may not be where we want to be—or even where we thought we'd be—after all these years.

Have you been in this position before? Do you feel like you're battling where you are now to get where you want to be? Do you know that where you are right now is not where you're going to be for the rest of your life?

This is the place where you embrace something called *The In-Between*, which is the title of the book by my friend and popular author Jeff Goins. It's in those moments of growing, waiting, learning, and stretching that we finally discover the truth that's inside us.

Look, the battle is the Lord's. You don't have to fight it alone. God understands that you might not be where you want to be right now. But while you're here, be the best you can possibly be. And be grateful. Don't murmur and complain. A grateful heart is a happy and healthy heart.

What about you? Are you in a place you know you're not destined to stay in? Do you feel there is something greater for your life? What is it?

_____

_____

_____

_____

_____

_____

_____

_____

12

*Why You Might Forget
Everything You Just Read*

You've made it this far, and we've determined that you are already more than enough to achieve your goals. You can start *today* to live a fulfilling, happy, and enjoyable life.

Isn't that how we want life, love, and work to be? Enjoyable? Fulfilling? Satisfying? In order for that to happen, though, we sometimes have to ruffle a few feathers, shake the boat, and cause an upset. Not everyone will be happy for you when you share your dream. And it's not always because they are "hatin" on you. Sometimes it's just because they are not for you.

Let me explain.

Would you go to a water fountain expecting Coca-Cola? Of course not. So, why do we go to people who are full of emptiness, bitterness, and regret in order to feed, fuel, and encourage our dreams? I once heard it said that there are three types of people in life, and they can be likened to parts of a tree: leaves, branches, and roots. People who are like leaves will change with the weather and be insecure, unstable, and moody. People who are like branches will invite you to put a little weight on them, but as soon as you do, they break. Roots are the ones who are stable, secure, and solid. Don't plant a leaf in the ground and expect it to become a root.

And then, some of us just get distracted. Webster's dictionary defines *distraction* as something that makes it difficult to think or pay attention. While not all distractions are bad, they are still all around us: e-mails, phone calls, appointments, more e-mails, errands, more calls. You get the idea. In his book *Rudder of the Day*, *New York Times* best-selling author Dan Miller says,

> In the busyness of modern life, I fear we have lost the rhythm between activity and rest. "I am so busy." We say this as a badge of honor, as if our exhaustion were a trophy, and our ability to withstand 70-hour weeks a mark of real character.
>
> We convince ourselves that the busier we are, the more we are accomplishing and the more important we must be. But is this really

so? Does more activity really mean more accomplishment? To be unavailable to friends and family, to miss the sunsets and the full moons, to blast through all our obligations without time for taking a deep breath—this has become the model of a successful life.

In his incredible book, *Essentialism, The Disciplined Pursuit of Less,* author Greg McKeown lays out a systematic discipline for discerning what is absolutely essential, then eliminating everything that is not, so we can make the highest possible contribution toward the things that really matter.

Here are some of my takeaways:

1) Have a Digital detox day. Turn off all media at a certain time each day.
2) Have a personal quarterly detox day where you get away and just enjoy nature. No electronics.
3) One day a week - vacate. If you can't do the entire day, take an hour or 30 minutes to do nothing. Rest your mind.
4) End your day at a certain time each day. The earlier the better. Spend more time with your family.
5) Become aware of the risks of success. Be careful of the undisciplined pursuit of more and the danger of becoming an "achievement junkie". Focus on what

you are uniquely and authentically called to that will make the greatest impact on others. You don't have to chase down every shiny new program or opportunity. Focus on the things that matter most.

Life is too short to rush through the things that matter most. We can be here today—and be gone today. Choose today to *become* not just to *do*. *Be* a friend. *Be* a sister. *Be* a daughter. *Be* a dad. Take a walk. Give thanks for simple things. Bless your children. Turn off the TV and cell phone every now and then and just *be*. Carve out time for restoration and spiritual rejuvenation. You're not being lazy. You're just being smart.

So, even though we all deal with distractions, decide today that you won't ignore the individuals who love you the most. At the end of the road, no one says, "I wish I had spent more time at the office or had answered more e-mails."

If your family is still living, you are tremendously blessed. Go hug your mom. Call your dad. Encourage your children. Forgive your enemies. Send your sister a card, and tell her you love her. Plant seeds of life now, for one day it will all be over. Dare to live your best life now!

Jeff Goins says, "The legacy of your life will not be judged by how many e-mails you responded to or how well you maximized your lunch break. It will be measured, I believe, by how interruptible you were."

Today, cherish the life you live. You have what it takes!

The world is not doing well, and it needs your voice desperately. You are someone who wants to live more than an average life, to do something important and leave a mark. You want your skills and talents to bring joy to others and to help them not to give up on their biggest dreams.

You have what it takes! Go for it! You have more people cheering for you than you realize. Don't cheat the world out of the book you will write, the organization you will start, or the friendship you will give. Sure, there will be people who will try to stop you and sabotage your success, but go for it anyway. Don't let anyone tell you that you can't do it. You will do it, and you can cross that finish line! Why? Because you're a fighter and you have what it takes. Fight on!

13

Make a Decision & Take Action

So, what's it going to be? Are you going to make a decision today to take a step in the direction of your goals? This is your season. You have to believe that and then *act* on it. Inspiration without action means little or no progress. The choice is yours. No one will build your dreams with as much fervor and diligence as you do. Start researching what it will take to make your goals a reality. If you're sincerely ready to go to the top and want help along the way, I'm ready to help you get there. Go to www.jevonnah.com to register for the next Deep-Dive VIP live training or to submit an application for one-on-one coaching.

Perhaps you still need help finding your purpose and owning your voice. You may feel overwhelmed and stuck. But we can switch that together. Here's the hope and the affirmation: I will personally hold you by the hand and help you get *massive* results.

If you don't have a website or a business plan, you need help building your brand or finding your authentic purpose, or you need further help in discovering what you were put on this earth to do, I'll walk through the process with you. I'll hold you by the hand and help you get *results*. The results, benefit, and value you get from having a private coach far exceeds the cost. I encourage you to visit www.jevonnah.com and click on "client testimonials" so you can read about the successes others are getting and what the power of walking in your God-given purpose can do. Because I put so much quality time and effort into my clients, and because of the follow-up and fresh content each client consistently receives, I only accept a small handful of clients at a time.

If you're interested you may send an e-mail to ladyj@jevonnahellison.com and request a prospective client interview.

Once your interview is approved, a proposal will be sent to you detailing what's in it for you, what you can expect at the end of the program, and current rates. This is an admission-only program. You must be approved for acceptance into the program. My private coaching is for high-potential people who are ready to elevate their influences, incomes, and impacts.

Imagine finally walking in your *true* calling and purpose, with more time for yourself and your family. It's time for you to live your dream. The kind of life you were meant to have awaits.

You'll also receive a **free** purpose guide, *"3 of the Best Ways to Get Crystal Clear on Your Purpose"* when you enter your name and email address at www.jevonnah.com You'll be joining a community of over 5,000 professionals who are committed to living with excellence and walking in their true God-given purpose.

14

Final Words from Lady J

Congratulations! If you made it all the way to this point, I celebrate you! You've been given a lot to think about in this guide, but now you have the knowledge to take the information you know and share it with the world. Here are just a few final thoughts I'd like to share with you before we finish up.

Keep God first.

Matthew 6:33 says, "But seek first the kingdom of God and his righteousness, and all these thing will be added unto you." Be the absolute best you can be at showing kindness and love. Pray always. Bind love and truth around your neck. Wear it to bed at night and when you wake up in the morning. You need a strategy when tough times come. Realize that trouble doesn't always last. You have what it takes to get through whatever you're going through. God is on your side. Remember that.

How much you succeed is all up to you.

(See Proverbs 4:10–15.) A wise man knows his strengths and weaknesses. He knows that he has to give control to God. Psalm 61:2 says, "From the end of the earth will I cry unto thee, when my heart is overwhelmed: lead me to the rock that is higher than I." Be like a stable thermostat. Just trust in the Lord. If you don't show God love in praise, you certainly won't show it in sacrifice and obedience. Proverbs 13:4 says, "The soul of the sluggard craves and gets nothing, while the soul of the diligent is richly supplied."

Speak life.

I must give credit to my darling mama, Dr. Rezine Keng. She gave me what I needed at a young age to succeed and have drive in this life. Ever since I can remember, she has always spoken life into me. She always told me that I could do all things through Christ, and she put the belief in me that I could do anything with God's help and grace. Even when things got tough and times were hard, she never faltered. She never gave up. She kept pressing, kept praying, and kept believing. I am eternally grateful and love her with all of my heart.

Don't worry about being perfect.

If you worry too much about getting everything just perfect, you'll stall your results and perhaps even stop them altogether. Just start! Take baby steps toward significant progress, day by day. Remember, an inch of progress is better than a mile of indecision.

Results don't come overnight.

There is no "magic button" that will get you significant results overnight. Success takes a lot of hard work, determination, and a willingness to learn. Give yourself a *chance* to succeed by giving yourself *time* to succeed.

Dan Miller says, "Success is never an accident. It typically starts as imagination, becomes a dream, stimulates a goal, grows into a plan of action – which then inevitably meets with opportunity. Don't get stuck along the way."

Don't be afraid to ask for help.

There is absolutely no reason why you shouldn't ask for help when you need it. Many people, including myself, are happy to help out. You'd be surprised at the resources available to you if you just ask.

Don't stop being awesome.

Never forget that for whatever project you decide to take on, you have what it takes!

Bonus

On my website is a quick-starter cheat sheet of the "must-have" resources I use in business. Just go to www.jevonnah. com and click on the resources tab for a free listing of tools to help you get started.

Remember Psalm 37:5: "Commit thy way unto the LORD; trust also in him; and he shall bring it to pass."

Internet Resources from My Personal Tool Box
This is an abbreviated list. For a complete list of books and resources I recommend, visit www.jevonnah.com

- www.johnmaxwell.com
- www.westa.com
- www.michaelhyatt.com
- www.nlcogic.org
- www.daveramsey.com
- www.48days.net
- www.acuff.me
- www.amyporterfield.com
- www.rayedwards.com
- www.goinswriter.com
- www.marshawnevans.com
- www.patflynn.com
- www.entreleadership.com
- www.marieforleo.com
- www.lisaterkeurst.com
- www.goingbeyond.com
- www.platformuniversity.com
- www.internetbusinessmastery.com
- www.chalenejohnson.com
- www.strengthleader.com
- www.brendonburchard.com

Bonus Reading

How to be Happy

Just yesterday, I had the incredible honor of spending one-on-one time with Pasty Clairmont, Best-Selling Author and phenomenal Women of Faith Speaker. My dear friend, Joanne Miller, an amazing Author, was also there and shared outstanding principles and stories that I'll never forget and impacted me for a lifetime.

Between bites of delicious pizza and seltzer, we shared stories about life, love and happiness. We talked about the ups and the downs and all the fuzzy moments in-between.

I had a chance to soak up tremendous amounts of wisdom from this talented woman who is full of God's love, humor and grace. Midway through the evening, I asked her a question:

"What is your definition of happiness, and are you happy?"

Now wait a minute, I thought to myself. 'This is Patsy Clairmont we're talking about here. Of course, she's happy!'

But something on the inside was tugging at me to ask. I wanted to learn from this giant of the faith who always appeared to have it all together, but I knew that nobody has it together all the time.

With her genuine smile and eyes that seem like they can go straight to the core issue in your soul, she responded in a powerful way that only she can and said something like (and I paraphrase):

"Oh honey, I've been so blessed to have a healthy balance of happiness and sadness in my life. I know what it's like to experience significant sadness, but yet to have extreme pockets of joy in-between those moments of sadness."

She emphasized the importance of being aware of those "pockets of joy." That's where happiness comes from. Happiness doesn't mean that everything is perfect and that we never have any problems. It's all about the perspective we choose to have and the way we choose to see the world.

Attitude is everything. We all hurt. We all go through pain. We all have a story.

But the choice is up still up to you. Either you can choose to live life as a victim and wish that life revolved around your pain, or you can use that pain as your roadmap to success.

If you are going through a difficult time right now, I empathize with you. My heart goes out to you. I pray for you. The Bible says to:

"Weep with those who weep and rejoice with those who rejoice." – Romans 12:15

But the Bible also says:

"Weeping may endure for a night, but joy comes in the morning." – Psalm 30:5

Here are 4 ways you can start practicing happiness today:

1) **Use your pain for purpose.** You aren't going through your pain for no reason. There's a bigger story. Use the lessons learned from your pain to help someone else.

2) **Use your rejection for direction.** Rejection hurts. It stings to the core. But just think how strong you are becoming because of it. Use that rejection to guide you into the next season God has for you. Minister and encourage someone else who is feeling rejected.

3) **Turn your mess into your message.** You have a story to tell. You have a message that the world needs to hear. Don't cheat the world out of the book you will write, the business you will start or the lives you will change. It's time to start now. Start before you're ready.

4) **Smile!** When you practice smiling (a REAL smile), it will do wonders for your mentality, attitude and relationships. You can't smile and think negative at the same time. Try smiling more!

Bonus

Just yesterday, I heard Copywriting Strategist, Ray Edwards talk about building your faith and ministering affirmations to yourself. Next time you're driving alone or are in front of the mirror, say these things and watch your day become brighter. Try saying them everyday to change your life!

- My prayers are powerful and effective
- I hear God's voice
- Today is the best day yet
- Everywhere I go, people encounter Jesus
- God is madly in love with me!

Question: How do you define happiness and are you living that out?

How to Deal with Overload

Can I be honest with you?

Yesterday I felt sincerely overwhelmed. Paper was sprawled everywhere across my desk and my inbox was flooded with email. Grocery shopping had to be done and calls needed to be returned. I had client applications to review and clients to coach (that's a good thing). Live events to plan and live events to attend. I was seriously dealing with information overload. And that was before it was 10 a.m.

Have you ever been there before?

I mean, it seems like there is always another good "thick" book to read, blog post to write, podcast to listen to, mastermind call to attend, PDF to download, webinar to register for, webinar to attend, replay to catch (or not), and email campaign to send out. And that doesn't include being a busy Pastor's wife. Yes, my life is busy to say the least.

But we're all busy. Every one of us, it seems, has too many things on our to-do-list every day.

It wasn't until I stopped and took inventory of my "why" that I was able to feel some relief. When you go back to your core of why you're doing business in the first place, you'll have a clearer perspective on what to say no and yes to.

So in thinking about how to deal with all of this information overload, I want to offer you 5 strategies that I hope will help you in your journey of online business and help you feel less stressed.

#1 Recognize that you can't do it all

More than likely, if you're reading this book, you're a high achiever who has an amazing track record of getting things done and pushing towards the next goal. But you're only one person. Don't overwork and neglect to take care of yourself. Get your rest. Eat whole foods. Drink more water. As you take care of yourself better, you'll have the energy to recognize those projects you should say no to. Get frazzled and you could easily end up saying yes to the wrong things just to feel productive.

#2 Revisit your "why"

Without a strong foundation, you'll run yourself into the ground trying to be all things to all people. No can do. Once you re-elevate why you're doing this in the first place, you'll be able to focus on those tasks that directly benefit your bottom line. Focus on doing 3 or 4 things with excellence

1,000 times. Not 1,000 things 3 or 4 times. This was a game changer for my business once I embraced this principle.

#3 Take baby steps

You can't eat the entire elephant in one day. Take Baby steps. In my Clarity Pack interview I did with Dave Ramsey's daughter, Rachel Cruze, she talks about the importance of Baby steps even for children when it comes to understanding money. Don't compare yourself to everyone else who may seem to be leaps and bounds ahead of you. Trust me, they got there by taking it one small step at a time.

#4 Set a Schedule

As entrepreneurs, we're always "on". Our minds are constantly thinking and strategizing about the next big thing. In order to control that heavy intake of awesomeness you get, set a schedule so your mind doesn't fade out due to overload. For example, you can say (and write down): "At 4:30 p.m., I'm shutting it down.No more email or Facebook." "From _____ to _____ (you fill in the hours) is my set time to:_____(be with my family, take my wife on a date, exercise, eat a healthy dinner, etc." The bottom line is that you have to tell your day where to go, not the other way around. Make time for margin, rest and to recharge your batteries. It really is that important.

#5 Ask for Help

As much as we want to read and take in excellent content everyday, we just can't do it all. So ask for help. Download apps like Audible to have audio books and blogs read to you while you commute. Invest in a virtual assistant to do your social media posting for you. Help is everywhere around us if you simply know how to ask.

A combination of these strategies will empower you to deal with information overload and feel less stressed. Hit that reset button, recharge your batteries and revisit the foundation of what matters most – your why.

And just in case you haven't heard it lately, I believe in you. You can do this. Hang in there.

An excellent book recommendation on this topic: Margin: Restoring Emotional, Physical, Financial and Time Reserves to Overloaded Lives by Dr. Richard A. Swenson

Question: How do you deal with overwhelm and overload?

What to Do When You Hit Rock Bottom

Life can be hard.

No, scratch that.

Life is hard.

It's also strikingly beautiful and full of "extreme pockets of joy" as my friend Patsy Clairmont, puts it.

But what happens when you don't see that beauty and joy? What happens when everyone around you is seemingly happy, and you're sitting there…trying to feel but still coming up empty?

What happens when you hit rock bottom?

We all have bad days. We may have days when we get up, get fully dressed, and then feel like crawling back in bed again. Rock bottom hurts. It's painful.

Your rock bottom may not be someone else's rock bottom. Fact is, we've all been at an extremely low point in our lives at one point or another. But here's the hope: You can only go up from here. Learn from this experience and grow like never before.

I don't know what you're going through today, or what you may be facing, but I want to encourage you with this thought:

Trouble won't last always.

I know it's tough right now and you may not be sure how this is all going to work out, but Jeremiah 29:11 says:

> 11 For I know the plans I have for you," declares the Lord, "plans to prosper you and not to harm you, plans to give you hope and a future.

Remember this. Your self-worth is not dependent upon your performance and others opinions of you. Even when others don't approve or accept you, know that you are still fiercely loved and accepted by God.

Instead of feeling like you have to be perfect or gain everyone's approval, remember that Christ justified you when you accepted Him. And if you haven't accepted Jesus Christ as your Lord and Savior and would like to do that now, feel free to send me an email to ladyj@jevonnahellison.com. I would be honored to pray with you.

Colossians 1:21-22 says, "Reconciliation means that although I was at one time hostile toward God and alienated from

Him, I am now forgiven and have been brought into an intimate relationship with Him. Consequently, I am totally accepted by God."

Here are 3 strategies for dealing with rock bottom moments:

1) **Calm down.** When you are anxious and full of stress, it's even more difficult to sort things out clearly. Take a walk, get away from the situation, and clear your head.

2) **Seek wise counsel and confide in a trusted friend.** Everyone doesn't need to know your business. Seek out those who have been through what you're going through, and actually got through it themselves with victory. Feelings that are left bottled up for too long can explode if not dealt with in a timely and wise manner.

3) **Pray.** Prayer works. James 5:16 says that the "effectual, fervent prayer of a righteous man availeth much."

When you hit rock bottom, remember that your blessing is closer than you think. The fastest way back up is down on your knees in prayer.

What have some of your rock bottom moments been and how did you get back up?

How to Graciously Say No when you Feel the Pressure to Say Yes

This morning, I received a fantastic email from Lysa TerKeurst. Lysa leads women in the adventure of faith and is a New York Times bestselling author and speaker. I joined in on her webcast last Tuesday and was tremendously blessed. Lysa is an excellent communicator and connector of people.

Have you ever said yes when you absolutely, positively knew that you should have said no?

I think we've all been there. Sometimes we experience guilt when we say no, and other times we say no while all the time thinking in the back of our minds, "what will she think?" "I should have said yes."

Saying no doesn't have to be hurtful. You will survive and so will the person you're saying no to.

In a book I read last summer called Boundaries by Dr. Henry Cloud & Dr. John Townsend, they talk about "calculating the cost" of our endeavors:

> So you were asked for something you weren't sure you had left over to give. You weren't sure you could do it with a "cheerful heart"

(2 Cor. 9:7). What happened next is what this particular boundary yardstick is all about. You probably did one of two things:

1. Since you were unsure, you said yes.
2. Since you were unsure, you said no.

Which is the more mature of these? In most cases, the second. Why? Because it is more responsible to give out of our resources than to promise that which we might not be able to deliver. Jesus said that we are to "calculate the cost" of our endeavors.

Suppose one of you wants to build a tower. Will he not first sit down and estimate the cost to see if he has enough money to complete it? For if he lays the foundation and is not able to finish it, everyone who sees it will ridicule him. (Luke 14:28-30)

Here are 10 ways to graciously say no that Lysa shared on her blog today:

Personal:

1) While my heart wants to say yes, yes, yes, the reality of my time makes this a no.
2) I am honored by your request but I'm in a season of refocusing my priorities and have committed not to add anything new right now.
3) After living at an unhealthy breakneck pace for too long, I'm learning to realistically assess my capacity. Though I would love to say yes, the reality of my limitations means I must say no this time.
4) I so appreciate you asking me, but I must be brave and decline this opportunity. Saying no is hard for me but necessary in this season. Thank you for understanding.
5) I've promised my family not to add any new commitments to my schedule right now. Thank you for our friendship that allows me to be honest with my realities.

Professional:

6) Thank you for thinking of me. Your project sounds wonderful. However, as much as I would love to be involved, I can't give your project the attention it deserves right now.
7) While I would love to connect about your new project, I've discovered this is one of those activities I must

give up while trying to _____
(write my book, start my business, stick to my project, etc.) Saying yes would just enable my unhealthy habit of procrastination. Thank you for understanding and helping me push through to the finish line.

8) There is nothing more that I love than helping others in my field get started. Unfortunately, I get so many requests for this that I'm no longer able to meet in person. So, I've created this attached document with my best advice. (Create a standard PDF for instances like this so you only have to type out your advice one time.)

9) While I don't have time for a lunch appointment, I'd love to connect for a few minutes over the phone. I can talk from 8-8:30am.

10) Thank you so much for caring enough about me to want my involvement. Unfortunately, I'm not able to participate this time. But I'm certainly cheering for your continued success.

For more encouragement to know when to say yes and how to say no, check out Lysa's new book, *The Best Yes: Making Wise Decisions in the Midst of Endless Demands.*

Question: Have you ever had a hard time saying no?

Imagine Doubling your Productivity and Success this Year

Have you ever wished there were more hours in the day to get things done?

Wished that you had more help to accomplish your daily goals and stay on track?

What would it feel like to finally achieve that weight loss goal? Be debt-free? Experience the freedom of truly walking in your God-given purpose?

Yesterday, I heard a fantastic podcast by Copywriter and Communications Strategist, Ray Edwards. He talked about "5 Bad Habits that will wreck your life."

The truth of the matter is that if we don't change our bad habits, realizing more hours in the day or achieving our goals will just be a dream. And a dream without a deadline is just a wish. You have to do more than wish. You have to take action.

Someone recently asked, "how do I balance business, family and ministry? I am determined, but it's challenging to complete projects."

Here's my answer:

You have to selectively choose the projects that will give you the greatest return for your time and investment. Balance is a misnomer. If someone is trying to do it all and make everyone happy, your goal is futile at best. You'll never be able to do everything and make everyone happy.

You must decide. When you say yes to one thing, you are inevitably saying no to other. The challenge is in saying yes to the best thing. And that's your choice to make. But here's the really good news: It will always be challenging to complete projects. Welcome to the world of high achievers and the top 5%. But you should embrace challenges as an opportunity for God to shine through you. Don't back down because of the obstacle, embrace it. Learn from it. Grow from it. And take action everyday...a single step forward everyday toward your goals.

Here are 7 steps to help you move forward:

1) **Surround yourself with the right people**. Be sure your associations are intentional. Hang around people who are successful or who are doing what you want to be doing. Ask questions. Learn from them.

2) **Get a coach.** The former CEO of Google, Eric Schmidt, recently said that every truly successful person has a coach. Even he has a coach. If you

are truly serious about your growth, business and success, invest in a coach.

3) **Read excellent books.**

4) **Listen to podcasts**. You have to feed your mind with excellence and quality everyday.

5) **Practice delayed gratification and a victorious mindset.** We live in a world of instant gratification. Practice saying no to the cookies and donuts this week. And next week too. Say yes to more exercise and drinking more water. Speak out loud to yourself that which you want to become.

6) **Invest in conferences.** I can't stress this enough. Surrounding yourself with like-minded people will shift your thinking and cause you to excel faster than ever.

7) **Stop watching so much TV.** Don't let television rob you of your time. Yes, entertainment is fine...in moderation. Instead of watching so much TV, read a book, write a book, go for a walk, spend time with your family, go to the gym, build something.

Question: Which of these 7 steps are you going to do right now to move you forward?

How to Live a Life you Can be Proud of and what I learned from a sweet lady named Ms. Sharon

2 weeks ago, I attended the Memorial Service for Ms. Sharon Lee.

Ms. Sharon, as she was affectionally called, volunteered in our church daycare. She was faithful, consistent, and funny. She was simply herself. I'll always love her for that.

She was 65, full of life, always had an encouraging word, and is gone much too soon.

Ms. Sharon had a laugh that could light up a room, a walk that could keep up with the best runway models, and a clever mind that would keep you guessing what she had up her sleeve next. :)

Although she was always building me up, giving me something sweet to munch on and saying something nice to me, her consistent love did not go unnoticed. While others may have discounted her contributions, I never let anyone say anything negative about her in my presence. She was the kind of person who loved you to the moon and back.

She lived a life that she could be proud of in the end, and there's so much I learned from her life. She'd be shocked to know I wrote an article about how her life impacted mine, but she is worthy of this and so much more. Here are 5 points that will help you to also live a life that you're proud of, no matter what other people may think.

1) **Humility** – Ms. Sharon didn't have any airs about her. None. She would speak to everyone that came to the daycare door and treat them with love and respect. No matter what kind of day they were having, she'd make them feel better. Adopt an attitude of gratitude to sharpen your humility and attract others to you.

2) **Humor** – There was never a dry moment with Ms. Sharon. She was always laughing. Always smiling. Being around her made the room light up. Try smiling and having negative thoughts at the same time. You can't do it. To have a better attitude, try smiling more.

3) **Honesty** - I'll never forget when Ms. Sharon got into a disagreement with one of the daycare workers. She came to my office in tears talking about what happened. She explained that she was crying because she didn't want to hurt the other person's feelings. I heard her out, listened, corrected the problem, and then walked from behind my desk, and just held her. That embrace I'll never forget. After that moment, I knew the honest truth about a situation would always come from her. Cultivate an environment of honesty by letting others know it's safe to be honest with you, and they won't risk losing your friendship.

4) **Heartfelt Love** - Ms. Sharon was a giver. She always had a bag full of goodies. I'll never forget one day she asked me what my favorite type of candy was. I told her "SEE'S Divinity Puffs". The next thing I knew, a box of Divinity Chocolates from SEE'S Candy Company was on my desk. Ms. Sharon genuinely loved me and her love made me want to give back to her. So the next time I went to California, I had to bring her a gift card to her favorite hamburger stand, In-N-Out. The small things matter more than you realize. Practice loving and leading the one's who matter most to you.

5) **Healing from Heartache** - Ms. Sharon had her fair share of heartbreak and heartache. She went through trials, tribulations, the storm and rain. Yet I never once saw her allow those storms to get the best of her. She'd find a way to get to church, ask for a prayer, or smile and laugh her way to a better tomorrow. Use your rejection for direction and your obstacles for opportunities.

Rest in peace, my sweetheart Ms. Sharon. Good night for now. I'll see you in the morning.

This post is dedicated to Ms. Sharon Lee and her loving family.

Love always,
Lady J

The Beauty of a Life Well Lived

Yesterday, our Head Deacon died.

It was an incredibly sad day.

His name was Roosevelt Calhoun.

He was a man of great honor and character. He was one of the few remaining mavericks of integrity left in our world today. In fact, his demeanor was as stately as the soaring eagle, yet free and strong as the wind beneath her wings.

The call came around 8:24 p.m. My husband and I rushed to the hospital to be with his wife and family.

We weren't the only ones.

There were crowds of people from the church and community gathered from all around the city to rally beside his loving wife & children. We grieved with them.

Romans 12:15 says to: "Rejoice with them that do rejoice, and weep with them that weep."

Deacon Calhoun left an incredible legacy behind. And that's what ends up happening, isn't it? When you live a life of integrity and honor, a legacy is forged. People want to be like you, and learn how they too can leave a remarkable legacy behind for their family and loved ones. Although it was a sad day, we do not grieve as those who have no hope. We know that if we live right, we'll see him again.

1 Thessalonians 4:13-18 says: "But I would not have you to be ignorant, brethren, concerning them which are asleep, that ye sorrow not, even as others which have no hope. For if we believe that Jesus died and rose again, even so them also which sleep in Jesus will God bring with him.

For this we say unto you by the word of the Lord, that we which are alive and remain unto the coming of the Lord shall not prevent them which are asleep.

For the Lord himself shall descend from heaven with a shout, with the voice of the archangel, and with the trump of God: and the dead in Christ shall rise first: Then we which are alive and remain shall be caught up together with them in the clouds, to meet the Lord in the air: and so shall we ever be with the Lord."

Here are 3 ways you can build a legacy & make a lasting difference in the lives of others:

1) **It starts with your attitude.** You'll hardly find successful people who leave a powerful legacy with a nasty attitude. Sure, we all have bad days, but if you want to make a difference in the lives of others, it's critical that you learn how to control your emotions and stay positive.

2) **Connect with others.** The ability to connect with others begins with understanding the value of people. You can't value people if you don't truly care about them first. Take time to listen and connect with other people.

3) **Be genuinely interested in others.** Talk more about others in a positive way and less about yourself. When you seek to be genuinely interested in the successes, failures, ups and downs of others, they'll never forget how you treated them. Look for ways to add value to others on a consistent basis.

Deacon Calhoun did all of these. He had a great attitude, connected with others and was genuinely interested in them. He was a giver from his heart.

Truly, heaven has one of the very best in the company of the King.

Rest in peace, Deacon Calhoun. We will forever love you.

This post is dedicated to Mother Dorothy Calhoun and the loving memory of her beloved husband, Deacon Roosevelt Calhoun.

The Importance of Speaking from Your Heart

So one of the first things I learned when building a platform was the importance of truly speaking from the heart. Yes, I'm a Leading Purpose Strategist and Leadership Coach to Champions. Yes, I absolutely LOVE my work and watching other people succeed. But it is my absolute joy to help professional women create lives of authentic purpose, happiness and integrity through the power of entrepreneurship and personal development.

Speaking from the heart not only creates vulnerability and trust, but it allows more women to connect. Women like you who are full of amazing potential, loves God and is on the brink of doing great things, but who may get stuck when fear gets loud.

No matter who you are, or where you might be in life right now, know that I value you, your life, and the gifts you offer to the world. I value what God is doing in and through you. My website and the resources offered is all about helping you live out your God-given purpose. I hope that by sharing my story, it will help you share yours. I choose to write from the perspective of someone who has been there before and can share from my own experiences.

Now I don't claim to be an expert and I certainly don't know it all. I've just been through a whole lot of mountains in my life and have had the opportunity to make many mistakes, have struggles, lessons learned and amazing successes along the way.

You see, nearly 8 years ago, I left everything I knew. Friends and a wonderful family I grew up with, a job I actually loved, and my home state of California. I got married and became an instant Pastor's wife to over 5,000 members. My husband is the Senior Pastor of 1 church in 8 locations in Alabama.

I definitely know what it's like to deal with major transition, change & transformation in your life. Have you ever been there before? Leaving the familiar for the unfamiliar? The known for the unknown? Maybe you're wanting to start your own business, write a book, or launch your own product. Maybe you're a minister's or Pastor's wife too. Maybe you have absolutely no clue what you're supposed to be doing with your life right now. It feels like you're just floating.

With God's help and a supportive, loving family, I've had more good days than bad. In fact, my days have been amazing. Not perfect, but amazing. Why? Because I wake up every morning with a heart full of gratitude for the gift of His grace and mercy along my journey.

What about you?

Have you ever had a lack of self-confidence when doing something brand new or felt the need for a greater sense of direction? Maybe you are searching for your unique value and calling. If that's you, I am here to empower, inspire and motivate you to live out your God-given purpose. I know what it's like to deal with transition and transformation, and I want to help you deal with yours.

Keep these quotes in mind:

> "Where God guides, God provides. Where God directs, God protects." - Bishop Charles E. Blake

> "God is re-positioning you for greater things." - Bishop T.D. Jakes

You are going higher! I have coaching programs available if you want to go farther, faster that my clients get real results from. Just read some of the testimonials and you'll see what I'm talking about. If you're ready, I'm ready. In the meantime, take advantage of the free resources and content at www.jevonnah.com to be inspired to go to your next level of success.

4 Joys to be Realized from Living Out Your God-Given Purpose

Have you ever seen someone who is lost and refuses to ask for directions? I'm pretty sure we all have. No matter how deep in the woods they get, they just won't stop and ask for help. Could it be pride? Embarrassment? Denial? An "I know this, thank you very much!" attitude? More like a combination of all four! So instead of asking for directions and getting help, this person just drifts deeper and deeper into "lost land" when they could have avoided all the drama in the beginning by simply asking for help.

God doesn't want you lost. Instead, He wants you to ask Him for help to live out your God-given purpose. Here are 4 Joys to be realized from living out the purpose God has for you. I hope they will empower you to seek God for your divine purpose. They can be yours to experience as you keep Him first.

#1 – Clarity

Nothing is more empowering than knowing what in the world you're put on this earth to do.

When you know what you're here for and what you're supposed to be doing with your life, opportunities come to you in abundance. So many people drift aimlessly through life, just letting life "happen" to them. I believe you are different. You want your life to matter. You want it to count for something. You want to make a difference, encourage, impact and inspire others. Clarity comes when you cut the clutter and focus on your mission in life.

Proverbs 3:6 says, "In all thy ways acknowledge Him, and He shall direct your paths." Ask God for direction and clarity. He will give it to you.

#2 – Balance

When you know your purpose, you don't have to try to scramble and do everything. You are very clear on what God has called you to do, and that creates balance. I love what Crystal Paine said in her book, Say Goodbye to Survival Mode:

"I'd rather do a few things well, have my priorities in order, and enjoy life than try to do 200 things poorly and have a stressed-out, exhausted, passionless existence."

#3 – Love

When you know your purpose, it spills over into your relationships. You are able to love your family, spouse and children well. You no longer seek your purpose from people, but you have it from God. That clears the clutter and noise of things that may distract you.

1 Corinthians 12:4-8 says: "Love is patient and kind; love does not envy or boast; it is not arrogant or rude. It does not insist on its own way; it is not irritable or resentful; it does not rejoice at wrongdoing, but rejoices with the truth. Love bears all things, believes all things, hopes all things, endures all things."

#4 – Focused Thinking

A clear purpose creates a focused mind. When you are busy doing what God has told and assigned you to do, you don't have time to think about the negative people, naysayers and dream killers. You are busy building the wall and won't come down. The goal is to be so focused on Kingdom business that you operate from a heart of generosity and kindness without thinking twice.

Philippians 4:8 says "Finally, brothers and sisters, whatever is true, whatever is noble, whatever is right, whatever is pure, whatever is lovely, whatever is admirable–if anything is excellent or praiseworthy–think about such things."

Question: What are some joys you are experiencing from living out your purpose?

When Daddy Walked Away

My dad walked away.

On Christmas Eve.

I was 7.

"Please Daddy! Please don't go! This is all my fault. I'll do better in school! I promise! Please just don't go," I cried, with the tears pouring down my cheeks.

But no matter how much begging or pleading my little 7-year-old self did, he left. On Christmas Eve.

I was hurt, angry and confused. All the way through college, Mama would always tell my sister and me to love, pray for and respect him. "That's your dad", she'd say. "You must forgive."

I didn't want to.

I was hurt. Deeply.

Even though the Bible says in Colossians 3:13 to forgive quickly, I definitely understood what it was like to go through a "slow forgiveness."

Dr. Meg Meeker, the country's leading authority on parenting, teens and children's health says that throughout the course of her lifetime, every woman will take at least 1 man to the grave, and it's not her husband. It's her Dad.

Either because she loved him so much and he passed away, or because he was just never there and she buried him in her heart.

My Story

I had buried him.

I wanted answers. Mainly, I just wanted to know why.

Why did the man I needed and wanted most in my life walk away? On Christmas Eve?

Time passed. I grew up.

By God's grace, I had several godly father figures in my life. But there was still a void for him — for my dad.

Not too long ago, I had a life changing experience when I came face to face with the pain of the memory that hurt me so deeply, so long ago.

It was at my Mastermind meeting with some of the most successful people in the world when a wise person began to ask me questions about my life. They asked me how I got so much confidence. I told them it was because of my Mom. Growing up, she always poured life into my sister and me, and told us that we were destined for greatness. She told me so much to the point where I believed her. I've been blessed with an extraordinary Mom.

Although their marriage wasn't perfect and they loved each other, they just couldn't live together. You can love someone, but just not be able to live with them.

But when this wise person asked about my Dad – that's when the tears started….and wouldn't stop.

You see, I hadn't told this story or even brought up the memory of that pain to anyone since I was 7. I wanted to bury it. Forget it. Leave it alone. Bury myself in work and my business. Act like it didn't bother me.

But it did.

It's wasn't until I came face to face with what hurt me the most and caused me the most pain that I was able to get free. It wasn't until I faced my rejection that I was able to use it for direction. It wasn't until I identified my pain that I was able to use it for purpose.

The Change

Fast forward to December 2014.

I have my answer.

Although he told me that it wasn't my fault growing up, as a kid, when your parents divorce, you just don't understand that. You feel somehow responsible for your parents' relationship – like there was something you could have or should have done to keep them together.

But I have my answer and have fully embraced it. Since I'm being honest here, let me just say I had my answer before. Dad had tried to explain what happened before. I just wasn't ready to receive it and still wanted to linger in my hurt and anger.

But this time, I was ready. I was ready because I've been through enough hurt, experienced enough hurt and have seen enough hurt to know that people aren't perfect and that true love forgives.

My answer was an apology.

Imagine that. An apology.

In so many words, what he said was "what I did, regardless of the circumstances, was wrong and I'm so sorry for the grief this has caused you."

All of a sudden the air felt different and a weight of over 25 years was lifted. It was all my heart needed.

I was free.

The Future

My Dad is a remarkable man, and today we have a wonderful relationship because of Jesus Christ. I've come to learn that he's super smart, and even won the Senior Olympics in his hometown recently. We laugh, talk and pray together. He is celebrating his 70th birthday next month, and I am going to honor him for the life and legacy he has lived.

He is completely fine with me sharing this message because in his words, "God uses the mistakes of our past to bring glory to His name. If by sharing our story others will be drawn closer to their dads and to the Lord, do it. It's all for His Glory."

The promise of Romans 8:28 is true. *"And we know that all things work together for the good of them that love the Lord, and are called according to His purpose."*

The promise of Genesis 50:20 and the story of Joseph is also true.

"As for you, you meant evil against me, but God meant it for good in order to bring about this present result, to preserve many people alive."

We all make mistakes. The world is bigger than my pain, my hurt and rejection.

By sharing this part of my story, the number of women (and men!) who have identified with it has been astounding. It has overwhelmed me with gratitude that these beautiful people trust me with their story and deepest hurts.

They want more. And to help and serve those who do, in 2015, I'm launching a 4-week online course called, **"When Daddy Walked Away" – How to use your Rejection for Direction.** *A 4-week online course for women who've been hurt because their dads walked off and left the family, but want to move forward.*

How This Can Help You

If you can identify with any part of this story, I want you to know that I understand. I get it. I know your silent struggle. I know how you bury yourself in success as you search for significance. I've been there. But please know that you're not alone.

Your father may have passed away, or you may be still estranged from him. God is able to touch your heart and cause you to not only forgive, but to be happy again.

Here are 3 ways you can use your rejection for direction:

#1 Tell it Usually it's that thing that you're most embarrassed or afraid to tell that will launch your business, ministry or relationships to the next level. When you're able to say it aloud and publicly, with honesty and raw truth, you'll experience a whole new freedom. A cleansing will begin to happen to you.

#2 Forgive it I know what it's like to go through a slow and painful forgiveness. But I've also learned that it's better to forgive quickly than it is to hold onto things in your heart. It will only make you sick. Talk about it. Get it out. Forgiveness is a process. Ask God for help in healing your hurting heart.

#3 Grow from it Once you've told it and forgiven it, use your story to help other people. After all, you went through what you did so that you can help someone else become a better and stronger person. Let God use you for His Glory!

To be notified of the launch of **"When Daddy Walked Away" – How to use your Rejection for Direction** *A 4-week online course for women who've been hurt because their dads walked off and left the family, but want to move forward* – you can subscribe to my blog at www.jevonnah.com

I wish you a life of happiness and healing.

My deepest thanks to my friend, Chuck Bowen of Chuck Bowen Coaching, for being that wise person who asked the right questions at my Mastermind meeting.

What I Learned from an Award from the United Nations

I'll never forget that moment I got the email from the UN. I was on the road headed to a Women's Conference. I was pouring out my heart to God. They were the kind of prayers you pray when you just don't know what to do, or the next step to take for that matter.

Have you ever felt like that?

Maybe it feels like you're doing everything you're supposed to be doing for your job, your health or even your relationships, but you just aren't seeing the kind of results you long for.

Perhaps the raise hasn't come yet and bills are stacking up. Maybe you're trying to lose the weight, but every time you get depressed, food is your comfort. Or perhaps your relationships are lacking the communication & vibrancy you once had, and you long to believe again. I have a message of hope for you today.

The Promise

"You have allowed me to suffer much hardship, but you will restore me to life again..." ~Psalm 71:20

In those moments of crying out to God, He heard me. In what to seem like a very long time, He heard me. He sent a word from across the nations to encourage me in the greatest way I could have ever imagined.

The Email That Changed My Life

My email pinged, and I glanced down for a quick moment (while stopped) and saw in the subject line something that said, **"Congratulations...from the United Nations..."**

I pulled over.

The letter went something like this:

"It has come to our attention that you have the heart and compassion towards others where you have exemplified "Treating Others the Way You Want to be Treated." Our office has come to know that you impacted your community with trust, dignity and have improved the quality of life by those you have touched through your humanitarian leadership.

Please accept our heartiest Congratulations on becoming one of our next recipients of the Golden Rule International Award. The award ceremony will be held publicly at the Gerald R. Ford Library Presidential Museum. Ambassadors to the United Nations in New York and The African Union will personally present the honors......"

Cue the tears.

My mourning was turned to joy.

This Took Me 2 Weeks to Post to Facebook

Soooo....I wasn't going to say anything about this until I had a chance to digest it myself. About 2 weeks ago, received a letter from an Ambassador to the United Nations.

Just found out that I was selected as a recipient of The 2015 Humanitarian Leadership Award – from the United Nations!!! The award is in honor Golden Rule Day – treating others the way you want to be treated.

Leaders from Capitol Hill will be presenting the award along with Kings and Queens from other countries and friends of the late Dr. Myles Munroe.

The grand ceremony is in April 2015 at the Gerald Ford Presidential Library in Michigan. I am so full right now. This is truly the Lord's doing. The United Nations!!!

#weserveaBIGGod! Coaching business going global. This award belongs to God!

Then I Came Back and Said This

I am overwhelmed with gratitude and thanks to God for all of you, my Facebook family and friends.

Your kind words and well wishes about my 2015 Humanitarian Leadership Award from the United Nations have been so generous.

While the comments have been wonderful, some have said that I deserve it. I know you mean well, but I do NOT DESERVE this honor. This award belongs to God and the people He's blessed me to serve.

If it had not been for the Lord who was on my side, I don't know where I'd be. HE ALONE is the one who gets the praise for this. I only mention it to bring glory to HIS name.

With hands upraised and my mouth filled with praise, God I love you and thank you for allowing me to walk in my authentic purpose to serve others. I love each of you! Thank you again! United Nations…here we come!!!

Here are 3 Ways You Can Practice More Gratitude Starting Today

1) Realize that it's not about you. The world is bigger than our rejection and hurt. We have so much to be grateful for. Take time to appreciate the small things – because to someone else, they aren't small at all. Learn how to use your rejection for your direction.

2) Change the company you keep. If you constantly hang around complainers and people who feel entitled to everything they have, one of 2 things will happen: either you will lift them up, or they will drag you down.

Make it easier on yourself and let your associations reflect people who are genuinely grateful for what they have.

3) Start writing handwritten thank you notes again. Perhaps you used to write handwritten notes but then life happened and you got busy, so you just shoot off a quick email instead.

Try getting into the habit of mailing a thank you note to someone who did something kind for you. It doesn't have to be a 5-page letter. Just something showing appreciation.

You'd be surprised how far small acts of thankfulness can go.

This post is in honor of my dear friend and sister, Jenny Lopez Ngigi, a national leader & extraordinary woman who reflects the Golden Rule everyday.

Question: Have you ever had a low moment and God sent someone or something to encourage you just in time? How do you show your gratitude?

THANK YOU

Thank you so much!

I hope you've enjoyed this book as much as I loved writing it for you. I can't thank you enough for your continued support of Jevonnah Ellison Leadership Coaching LLC and everything I do.

I sincerely appreciate each and every one of you for taking time out of your day or evening to read this, and if you have an extra second, I would love to hear what you think about it.

Please leave a comment and subscribe at http://jevonnah.com. If you don't do so already, you can follow me on Twitter (@JevonnahEllison) and join in on the Professional Women of Integrity Facebook fan page (www.facebook.com/jevonnahellison). It's completely free to join.

Thanks again, and I wish you nothing less than the best. Remember, you have what it takes!
Dr. Jevonnah "Lady J" Ellison
Your Leading Purpose Strategist & Leadership Coach, Speaker, Author, Happy Pastor's Wife
ladyj@jevonnahellison.com

AVAILABLE SEMINAR TOPICS

Here are some of my most popular keynote speaking topics and workshop requests. To submit a request for your speaking event, please visit www.jevonnah.com

Most Requested Speaking Topics & Seminars

Define Your Purpose and Find Your Authentic Voice: How to Develop a Personal Mission Statement That Changes the World

Imagine how focused you could be if you had a mission statement for your life. Having a clear outline of what's most important to you, what you want to achieve, and, ultimately, who you want to become can lead to a more rewarding life and career. Lady J has taught hundreds of people how to develop their own personal mission statements. This powerful workshop of self-discovery will guide you through a process to complete a personal mission statement and a value proposition, which will forever change the way you work, lead, and live your life. As a result of this session, you will:

- discover how your core values shape your approach to work, leadership, and life;
- raise the quality of your relationships, leadership style, and work performance;
- increase the level of satisfaction in your personal and professional life;
- begin to work with greater clarity, purpose, and productivity; and
- love your life again!

Powerful Goal-Setting That Glories God: Seven Steps to Start Living Your Best Life Now

It takes courage, determination, and a whole lot of hard work to start realizing your dreams. But take courage because, believe it or not, the journey starts in your mind. Change your thinking, and change your life. You've got to get out of your own way so you can stop making excuses and sabotaging your own success. This session will teach you how to get rid of negative thinking and unproductive thoughts and to reclaim God's authentic purpose for your life.

During this training, participants will discover:

- why it's so important to figure out your true purpose in life, and how to live that out;
- how to overcome the top five negative thought patterns that may be holding you back from living your ideal life; and
- a set of seven practical, proven strategies and tools to help you make progress on your goals.

Ready, FIRE!, Aim - Five Steps to Start Getting Paid to Do What You Love

Are you ready to transition from having a fun hobby to starting a real business? If you already have a business idea but you've been procrastinating on putting yourself "out there" for far too long, this workshop is for you! In this training, you will learn how to implement Lady J's seven-step system to get your business off the ground. This interactive workshop will equip you with the confidence, inspiration, and direction you need to launch your business this year. Lady J will teach you her own personal "Ready, **Fire**, Aim!" approach that gets results.

You will discover:

- why you *don't* have to have all your ducks in a row to launch your business;
- how to "bootstrap" your business, even when you don't have enough money to start;
- the secret to shifting your mind-set and eliminating limiting beliefs that are holding you back from getting paid to do what you love;
- how to manage your time so you can overcome procrastination and stay focused on your business goals;
- the ten different streams of income you can create based on your passion, skills, expertise, and experience; and
- the five essential steps you can take now to get your business off the ground this year.

How to Successfully Blend Ministry and the Marketplace: Seven Key Strategies You Can Put to Work in Your Business Now

So, you're in the ministry *and* you have a business? Congratulations! You are set apart and called for such a time as this. But have you ever wondered how to get paid by people who are used to receiving your services for free? Have you ever struggled with knowing what to charge, how to charge, and when to start? You're not alone. This workshop will empower you with the tools, strategies, and confidence you need to finally start acting like a real business.

In this seminar you will:

- learn how to position yourself strategically in the marketplace;
- realize the three critical tools every business person needs to sell anything;
- understand how loving your audience and clients opens new doors for you; and
- role-play the seven key strategies with other like-minded businesspersons so that you're positioned for your next client or customer

Business Women and the Holy Spirit: Why Every Businesswoman needs the Power of God in her life

Without God, we can do nothing. It is only by the grace of God that we are able to operate in business effectively and with integrity. Ministry and business **can** blend together beautifully. However, without the power of the Holy Spirit, which gives us the power to lead lives of character and honor, it is extremely difficult to do this on our own. This is why I teach the power of the Holy Spirit to young women and the positive impact of God's presence in their lives.

You'll be empowered, equipped, and enabled to:

- understand that the Holy Spirit is a gift to the believer that is freely given when asked for;
- finally gain an understanding of what it means to speak in your heavenly language;
- ask God for a refilling and refreshing of His power and anointing; and
- get motivated more than ever to make powerful strides in your personal and professional life.

What You Can Expect

1) Professional, prompt replies to your phone calls and e-mail messages
2) An announcement about your event on my blog and social media channels (assuming that your event is open to the public and you want additional visibility for it)
3) A personal phone consultation so we can better understand how I can best serve you and your audience
4) A professionally prepared presentation focused on the outcomes you want with your audience.
5) For God to have His way!

CONTINUE THE CONVERSATION

Connect with Dr. Jevonnah "Lady J" Ellison through the following venues:

Website: www.jevonnah.com
Facebook: facebook.com/jevonnahellison
Twitter: @JevonnahEllison

To see Dr. Jevonnah "Lady J" Ellison live, or to schedule her for your next event, visit www.jevonnah.com. Click on the speaking tab.

For consultation and coaching services, check out www.jevonnah.com. Click on the coaching tab.

For live events, visit www.jevonnah.com. Click on Register for a VIP Day.

Acknowledgments

My Lord and Savior, Jesus Christ

You are the reason for everything I do. Without you, I can do nothing. You get the glory! It all belongs to you. I love you with all of my heart.

My Husband, Pastor Terry Ellison

Thank you for supporting me through the birthing process of this book. I could feel your constant prayers and they meant so much to me. I love you.

Mom, Dr. Rezine Keng

You are the one who gave me confidence to achieve my dreams. You were always there. It's because of your prayers and love that I am where I am today. I didn't get here by myself. Your love saw me through it all. I can truly say that you are the most incredible woman I have ever known. You are wise, beautiful and strong. Thank you for loving me Mama. God gave me His **best** angel for a Mom. You have set an extraordinary example for me. Thank you for living a life of excellence and teaching me about faithfulness, love and integrity. This one's for you. I love you forever.

My Family

Dad, Eileen, Telicia, Jemar, Isaac, Ma & Pa Wrench, Nadie Conedy: I love you all from the bottom of my heart. Thanks for pushing me and believing in me

My West Angeles Family: Thanks for being there and for your lasting friendship. My family forever! And a special thanks to West Angeles Bible College, Judy McAllister, Augustine Hughes, Voice of Hospitality (love you Janice!) and my *entire* West Angeles Staff family. You all are the best!

My New Life Family: Thank you for your love, prayers and support. I value each of you!

Westbow Press

Special thanks to Shaun Kaffman, my check-in coordinator, Andrew of content editing, Adam Tinsley of publishing and Christine Moore, Editor and the entire team at Westbow/ Thomas Nelson for helping me with this project. We did it! Special thanks to Lois Russell for reviewing the very first draft and Fallone McQueen (FMA Graphics) and Dave Whitlock (Principle Design) for the cover design inspiration.

Bishop Charles E. Blake & Lady Mae

You saw potential in me before everyone else. Thank you for believing in me, supporting me and teaching me about what it meant to have a real relationship with God.

Dr. Barbara McCoo Lewis

You truly live out what a Proverbs 31 woman looks like. Thank you for pushing me and believing in me all these years. I love you.

Kathleen Kennedy

I'll never forget the seeds of life you sowed into me even at a very young age. Your believing in me made me want to be great. I'll never forget you.

Kim Blake Ludlow

Your lasting and genuine friendship has been a true God-send to me. I love you with all of my heart.

Very special thanks

Pat Flynn & Ray Edwards, Michael & Gail Hyatt-Platform University, Dan & Joanne Miller-48 Days, Dave Ramsey, Darren Hardy & SUCCESS, Brendon Burchard, Marshawn Evans, John Maxwell, Suzanne Evans, Les Brown, Patsy Clairmont, Amy Porterfield, Jim Rohn, Jon Acuff, Maria Andros & Jeff Goins. Thank you for everything you've done, directly and indirectly, to help me succeed.

48 Days Mastermind Thank you for your feedback and unwavering support of this project. I value each of you!

Thrive Mastermind, John, Athena & Michael - Thank you for being who you are... together for such a time as this.

Notes

Notes

Notes

Notes

Notes

Notes

Notes

Notes

Notes

Notes